Investigating
Forces and Motion

Jane Weir, MPhys

Physical Science Readers:
Investigating Forces and Motion

Publishing Credits

Editorial Director
Dona Herweck Rice

Creative Director
Lee Aucoin

Associate Editor
Joshua BishopRoby

Illustration Manager
Timothy J. Bradley

Editor-in-Chief
Sharon Coan, M.S.Ed.

Publisher
Rachelle Cracchiolo, M.S.Ed.

Science Contributor
Sally Ride Science

Science Consultants
Michael E. Kopecky,
   Science Department Chair,
   Chino Hills High School
Jane Weir, MPhys

Teacher Created Materials

5301 Oceanus Drive
Huntington Beach, CA 92649-1030
http://www.tcmpub.com
ISBN 978-0-7439-0573-2
© 2007 Teacher Created Materials, Inc.
Made in China
Nordica.112016.CA21601787

Table of Contents

Forces Make Things Happen!

Without forces, the world would be a very boring place. Nothing would happen at all!

A **force** is a push or pull or twist that usually causes movement. Forces cannot be seen, but their effects can be seen. Forces can make objects move, speed up, slow down, turn, change direction, or change shape.

You use forces all the time. The force of your muscles on your bones makes you move. When you kick a football, the force on the ball makes it move. Your weight is a force. It pushes down on the earth.

Forces are even acting on things when they are still. For example, a swing that isn't moving is being affected by two important forces. **Gravity** (GRAV-i-tee) is a force that is pulling the swing down. At the same time, the chain or rope pulls it back up.

Forces move your body and the soccer ball and keep the swing where it is. Forces even keep the Moon in the sky!

A force called the strong force keeps atoms together. Without forces, the universe would be a big soup of lost particles.

The unit of force is the **newton** (N). It is named after Sir Issac Newton, an important scientist and mathematician born in 1642. Newton wrote the rules that describe the effects of forces. He showed that gravity is the same force whether it makes an apple fall from a tree or keeps planets in their orbits.

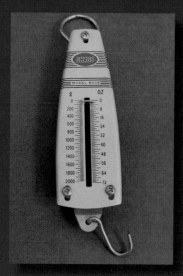

Measuring Forces

Forces can be measured using a Newton Meter (also called a spring scale). A Newton Meter has a spring in it. The more force that pulls on the spring, the more it stretches.

Moon Diet?

Mass is the amount of "stuff" (called matter) from which something is made. Your mass is the same wherever you are in the universe. Your weight is the force that gravity exerts on your mass. On the moon, gravity is one-sixth of the strength it is on Earth. So, if you were there, your mass would be the same as always, but your weight would be only one-sixth of that on Earth. So, a person who weighs 100 pounds (444 N) on Earth will weigh about 16 pounds (71 N) on the moon.

Simple Machines

Machines can be used to make work easier. For example, **levers** are one kind of simple machine. They make it easier to do work by multiplying the force put into a job. A seesaw is a lever. A lever works by using force to make objects turn around a **pivot** point called a fulcrum (FULL-krum). Longer levers make life easier because they produce a greater turning force about the pivot.

Other simple machines are the pulley, wheel and axle, inclined plane, screw, and wedge. These simple machines can be combined to make more complex machines like the bicycle. There are many more machines. You use them every day. Did you open a door today? If you did, then you used a machine.

↑ lever

A seesaw is a lever. Your arms and legs are levers, too!

How Do Brakes Work on a Bike?

If you looked at a flat surface with a microscope, you would see that it's not really flat. All surfaces have bumps and edges. This means that, when you pass them over one another, they don't slide as smoothly as you'd think. All the teeny bits on the surfaces bump and catch on each other. This makes the particles (PAR-tuh-kuhls) in the surfaces move about more.

Rubbing produces heat. Heat is just movement of tiny particles that make up substances. So, the substances get hotter. The energy of movement (kinetic energy) is changed into heat energy. This means there is less kinetic energy left. The thing that was rubbing or moving goes slower than before. It has less energy to move. So, when you apply brakes, the energy lessens. That is how braking slows you down.

The force at work here is called **friction**. Turn to page 14 to learn more about it.

Speed, Velocity, and Acceleration

Speed is how far something moves in a given time. It is measured in distance per unit of time. **Velocity** (vuh-LOS-uh-tee) is speed in a specific direction. It is also measured in distance per unit of time. If an object is traveling at the same speed in a straight line and you know how far it has traveled, then you can figure out its velocity. Take the distance traveled and divide it by the time taken to travel. Then you have the velocity.

Acceleration (ak-sel-uh-RAY-shun) is how much the velocity of an object changes in a certain time. It is measured in meters per second squared. To accelerate means to speed up. **Deceleration** is the opposite of acceleration. To decelerate means to slow down.

A Kick in the Pants

Sometimes fighter pilots accelerate their planes so fast that the force created makes all the blood run from their heads and into their legs. To stop this, they wear special pants called "anti-g trousers." The g stands for gravity caused by acceleration. The pants press on their legs to stop the blood from running into them.

◀ When a racecar pulls ahead of another car, it is accelerating.

Funny Face

When stunt pilots like the Blue Angels fly their planes in a loop-the-loop, the skin on their faces becomes temporarily distorted. That is because their skin is being accelerated. The face skin is not attached to anything, so it gets pushed out of shape.

Balanced Forces

More than one force can act on an object at once. When this happens, there is something like a tug-of-war between them.

If all the forces that act on an object are balanced, then the object will stay still or keep doing what it was doing. When the forces are balanced, we can say that the object is in **equilibrium** (ee-kwuh-LIB-ree-uhm). An example of this is a light hanging from the ceiling. The downward force of the light's weight is balanced by an upward force from the cord. The light stays still.

Other examples of equilibrium are a football lying on the ground or an apple on a tree. In fact, any object at rest is in equilibrium. A floating boat is in equilibrium, too. The upward thrust of the water balances its weight and stops it from sinking.

⬆ This boat has equal forces from gravity (down) and the water (up), so it is in equilibrium.

⬇ Until one side exerts more force than the other side, a tug-of-war is balanced, or in equilibrium.

GUT

Scientists are trying to find a way to describe the universe that links all the different forces together. They call this the Grand Unified Theory or GUT. They haven't found one that works yet. But they're still looking!

If the forces on an object are not balanced, then the object will change speed or direction. For example, when a ball is kicked, the kicking foot provides a force that changes the balance. When a child is pushed on a swing, the pusher's hand provides the force. When a tennis ball is hit, the force is provided by the racquet.

▲ This athlete provides force to the ball.

Objects standing still will start to move in the direction of the force. Objects that are already moving will either change direction, speed up, or slow down. The bigger the force, the more the object accelerates.

This makes sense. If you push something hard, then it will speed up much more than if you just give it a little tap. If you pedal really hard on your bike, then you will speed up much more than if you just push the pedals gently.

When Is a Juggling Ball Traveling Fastest?

Velocity is greatest when the ball leaves and approaches the hand. It is least at both the very top of its path and when it is actually in your hand. Its velocity is zero for a split second at these points when it changes direction.

On the way down, the acceleration on the ball comes from gravity. On the way up, gravity is still trying to accelerate it downwards and will act to slow the ball down until it stops at the top. As it is just about to leave your hand, the acceleration on the ball is greatest because your hand is delivering an upward force to it.

▲ For a skydiver, gravity and air resistance balance out at 195 km/h.

Friction and air resistance are forces, too. Friction is a force that acts on surfaces to slow things down or stop them from moving. Air resistance is an upward force that slows falling objects. So, both forces cause moving objects to slow down. And they always act against the direction of motion. For example, a boat is slowed by pushing against water. A parachute slows down a skydiver. The force that acts against the movement of an object such as the parachute is called drag.

Friction can be useful. It is needed for walking, because it provides grip between the ground and a person's feet. Friction is needed to pick up objects that would otherwise just slip out of your hands. Tires need friction to grip the road. Without friction, it would be like riding on slippery ice.

Sometimes friction is not so useful. Friction between machine parts and gears leads to wear and tear. Friction between moving parts on machines causes parts to grate over each other and heat up. This makes them less efficient.

Friction Addiction

Rock climbers use forces to stay on the rock. Friction between the climber's hands and feet and the rock stops the climber from sliding or falling off. The upwards force from the hands and feet balances the downward force of gravity. Also, the climber can wave a foot or hand to one side for balance while leaning the other way. Rock climbers wear sticky, flexible rubber shoes. This gives them a lot of friction between their shoes and the rock.

Fishy Fact

Objects moving through water experience more friction than objects in air. Water is denser than air. The reason fish and other sea creatures like dolphins are so smooth is that the quality of smoothness lowers friction between their bodies and the water.

Newton's Laws of Motion

A scientist named Newton wrote about forces and motion. Today, we use three laws named after him. The First Law of Motion describes objects in equilibrium. It is called the law of **inertia** (in-UR-shuh). Inertia means resistance to a change in motion. Here is Newton's first law:

A body will stay in a state of rest or uniform motion in a straight line until acted on by an outside force.

In other words, if you don't push, pull, or squeeze something, it will carry on as it was. Objects at rest will stay still. For example, a leaf that falls from a tree will stay

▲ Isaac Newton

◀ Newton's Laws of Motion apply to everything— even baseball!

where it lands on the ground unless wind, an animal, or a person moves it. Moving objects will carry on moving in a straight line at the same speed. If you hit a baseball, it would go on forever in a straight line if gravity, drag, or someone catching it didn't get in its way.

Newton's Second Law of Motion is the law of acceleration. It describes what happens when force is used:

The acceleration of a body is directly proportional to the force acting on it and is in the same direction as the force. The acceleration is also inversely proportional to the mass of the body.

This means that if a force is applied to an object, then the object will always move in the direction in which the force is acting. The harder it is pushed, the more it will speed up. For example, when you hit that baseball, the force you exert on it through the bat accelerates the ball in the direction you hit it. The harder you hit it, the faster it goes.

▲ Dr. Trachette Jackson

Math, Then and Now

In order to do his work, Newton started a new branch of math. It is called calculus. Calculus is important for every scientist. Dr. Trachette Jackson uses it in her field of mathematical biology. That is the study of math in living things. She is using calculus to help study cancer cells. The more she knows, the closer she comes to stopping them. So, Newton's important work then helps Jackson's important work now.

Well, Blow Me Down!

Newton's second law explains why leaves are blown around more than sticks are. A leaf can catch a lot more wind than a stick can. The more wind, the more force, the more motion!

Newton's third law describes the reaction force. The Third Law of Motion is the law of action and reaction:

For every action there is an equal and opposite reaction.

The reaction force pushes back against objects. This law explains why objects stay where they are instead of going crashing through the floor. You can feel the reaction force if you push against the wall. The pressure you feel on your hands is the force exerted by the wall on your hands. You can feel the reaction force when you sit on a chair. The reaction force pushing up balances your weight pushing down. The reason you can feel the chair under you is because of the reaction force.

The reaction force is how rockets are propelled through space. The rocket pushes a mass of burnt fuel out the back. The force of the rocket on the burnt fuel is the same as the force of the burnt fuel on the rocket. The two push each other apart, which makes the rocket go forward.

◄ The Space Shuttle uses Newton's Third Law to reach orbit.

Why Do Planes Need a Runway to Take Off?

An airplane wing is curved. As a plane goes along the runway, air flows over and under the wing. Because the wing is curved, the air flowing over the top flows a longer distance than the air underneath.

So, the air is spread out on the top, causing it to have less pressure than the air below. This makes the air underneath push upwards and lift the wing. The faster the plane goes forward, the more this happens. Airplanes speed along a runway to catch lift.

The First Rocketeers

The Chinese invented rockets. Rockets need a force to propel them into space. The Chinese used gunpowder to power rockets as far back as 1150.

Air spread out = Less pressure

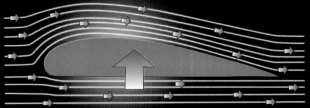

Air close together = More pressure

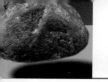

Gravity

Gravity is a force. It is different from most other forces because it can only pull things together but can't push them apart.

Gravity acts on mass. Gravity is what holds us on Earth and stops us from floating off into space. It also keeps Earth in its orbit around the sun. So, it stops Earth from floating off into space, too. Earth's gravity also keeps the moon in orbit around the planet. Without gravity, things would be floating around everywhere in space.

Newton was the first person to realize that the force making the moon orbit Earth is the same force that makes things fall to Earth. But scientists are still trying to figure out why gravity can only pull things together and can't push them apart.

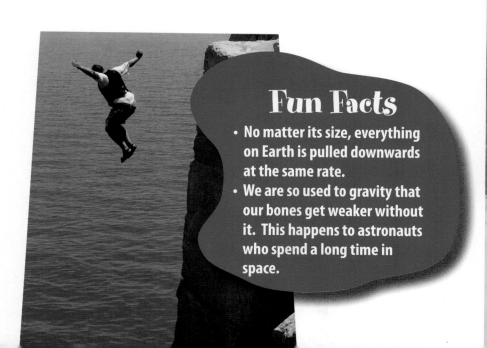

Fun Facts
- No matter its size, everything on Earth is pulled downwards at the same rate.
- We are so used to gravity that our bones get weaker without it. This happens to astronauts who spend a long time in space.

Falling

On Earth, things look like they are falling downwards. Actually, they are falling towards the center of Earth. If you could dig a hole through Earth, right out to the other side, and then jump down it, you would only go as far as the center of the planet. That is where gravity wants to take you.

▲ Without the force of gravity you would simply float off the planet!

More Mass Is Better for Gravity

Everything with mass produces a gravitational (grav-uh-TAY-shuh-nuhl) field. Even everyday objects have gravitational fields. But the force in most of these fields is so small that it doesn't have any effect we can see. It is so small that it doesn't make anything move.

The size of the attraction between objects depends on their masses. The greater their masses, the more they attract each other and the bigger the force that attracts them. For example, Earth's pull on the moon is very strong compared to the pull of two pool balls on a pool table. Earth's pull is much bigger than the pull between you and a friend.

The size of the force (how much things attract each other) also depends on the distance between the objects. The farther away objects are, the less they attract each other.

Objects with small masses have small gravitational fields. Because of this, their gravitational attraction is also small.

Doin' an Ollie

Have you ever done an ollie on a skateboard? If you have, you were using physics! All skateboard stunts – even just riding a skateboard – need the use of force to make them happen. To do an ollie, force from three sources is used. The first is the rider's foot pushing down on the tail of the board. This pushes the front of the board up. The second is the ground's reaction when the tail hits the ground. This pushes the back end of the board up. The third force is the rider's foot moving up the board. This tips the board forward so it can land flat at the end of the trick. Without any of the three forces, the rider wouldn't get anywhere at all.

Electricity and Magnets

Similar to the force of gravity, magnets exert a force on other magnetic (mag-NET-ik) materials without having to touch them. The closer the magnet, the bigger the force. Only some types of materials are magnetic. These include iron, steel, nickel, and cobalt.

Magnets are surrounded by an invisible field called a **magnetic field**. The magnetic field around a magnet can be seen with iron filings. Try putting a bar magnet, which is a magnet that has a long, thin rectangular shape, under a piece of paper. Then sprinkle iron filings on top. The filings line up along the field lines. You can see what happens in the illustration below.

Magnets have two poles called the north pole and the south pole. Opposite poles attract each other. Poles that are alike repel each other. Magnetic poles can't exist separately. Wherever there is a magnetic north pole, there is always a south pole. It is impossible for north and south poles of a magnet to exist by themselves. If you break a permanent magnet in half, it will become two smaller magnets. Each will have its own north and south poles.

▲ These iron filings align themselves along the lines of magnetic force around the red magnets.

◄ A compass shows direction by using a magnetic needle.

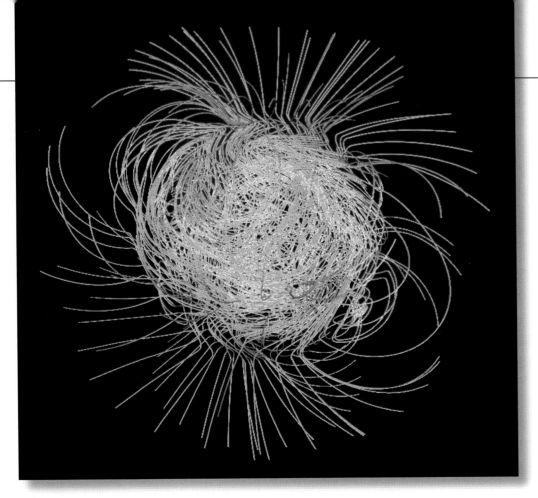

This image illustrates the magnetic north and south poles of Earth.

Earth's Magnetic Field

If a magnet is hung from a string or floated on a piece of wood on water, then it will swing around so that one end points north and the other south. This is because Earth has its own magnetic field, which attracts the suspended magnet. Earth's magnetic field acts like a giant bar magnet. This is why a compass works.

Electromagnetism

Electricity (uh-lek-TRIS-uh-tee) and magnetism are related. Because of this, their properties are sometimes grouped together. This is called **electromagnetism** (uh-lek-troh-MAG-ni-tiz-uhm).

Electromagnets are a good example of how electric and magnetic forces affect each other. They work because wires carrying electric current have a magnetic field around them.

An electromagnet can be made with a battery and a coil of wire. It has a north and south pole, just like a bar magnet does. A core of iron, like a nail, increases the strength of the electromagnet.

Fun Fact

A very strong electromagnet is used in Magnetic Resonance Imaging (MRI) scanners, which see inside the human body.

What's That Static?

Stereos make a buzzing noise when mobile phones are used near them because of electromagnetic interference. The electromagnetic field made by the mobile phone changes the electrical signal in the speakers.

They're Everywhere!

Electromagnets are used in many devices such as doorbells, security locks, metal detectors, and fish tank pumps!

⬆ This is an example of an electromagnet.

Materials

- stopwatch
- a piece of string 1.25 meters long
- 50 grams of play clay (plasticine)
- a laboratory stand and clamp, or sticky tape and a table or door frame
- sheet of paper
- marker

Procedure

1 Cut a piece of string to 1.25 meters.

2 Make a pendulum by molding a lump of plasticine onto the end of the piece of string.

3 Measure 1 meter up the string from the center of the plasticine blob. Put a mark on the string. Tie it to the stand and clamp it at the 1 meter mark. If you are doing this at home and don't have a stand and clamp, then you can tape the pendulum to a table edge or door frame.

Field Strength

4 Hold the pendulum blob to one side. Get ready with the stopwatch.

5 Let go of the pendulum and start the stopwatch.

6 Count 10 full swings (stopping point and back) of your pendulum. Then, stop the stopwatch when it arrives back at the start for the tenth time.

7 Record the time the pendulum took to make 10 swings.

8 Shorten your pendulum to .5 meters and repeat the experiment.

9 Figure out the time in seconds for one swing by dividing the time for 10 swings by 10. This is called the period of the pendulum.

10 Record your results in a table like the one shown here.

11 With the period you calculated (the time for one swing of the pendulum) in Step 9, find the force of gravity. You will use this formula:

gravity = (39 x length) / (swing time x swing time)

Calculate the gravity for each of the two pendula you made. It's tricky, but you can do it!

How do the values for gravity compare? What effect does changing the length of the pendulum have on the period?

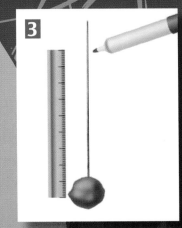

10

Pendulum Length	Time for 10 Swings	Time for 1 Swing
1 m		
0.5 m		

Glossary

acceleration—rate of change of velocity; speeding up

deceleration—slowing down

drag—the force that acts against the movement of an object

electromagnetism—electricity and magnetism combined

equilibrium—balance

force—a push or pull that can make things move

friction—force that acts on surfaces in contact and slows them down or stops them from moving

gravity—force that makes planets orbit the sun and holds objects on Earth

inertia—resistance to motion

levers—simple machines that make work easier by multiplying the force put into it

magnetic field—the area where magnetic force can be detected

mass—amount of matter something is made of

newton—a unit of force

pivot—a fixed point supporting something that turns or balances

speed—rate of motion or progress

velocity—speed in a certain direction

Index

Sally Ride Science™ is an innovative content company dedicated to fueling young people's interests in science. Our publications and programs provide opportunities for students and teachers to explore the captivating world of science—from astrobiology to zoology. We bring science to life and show young people that science is creative, collaborative, fascinating, and fun.

Image Credits